FACTS from OUR PLANET

An imprint of Om Books International

Contents

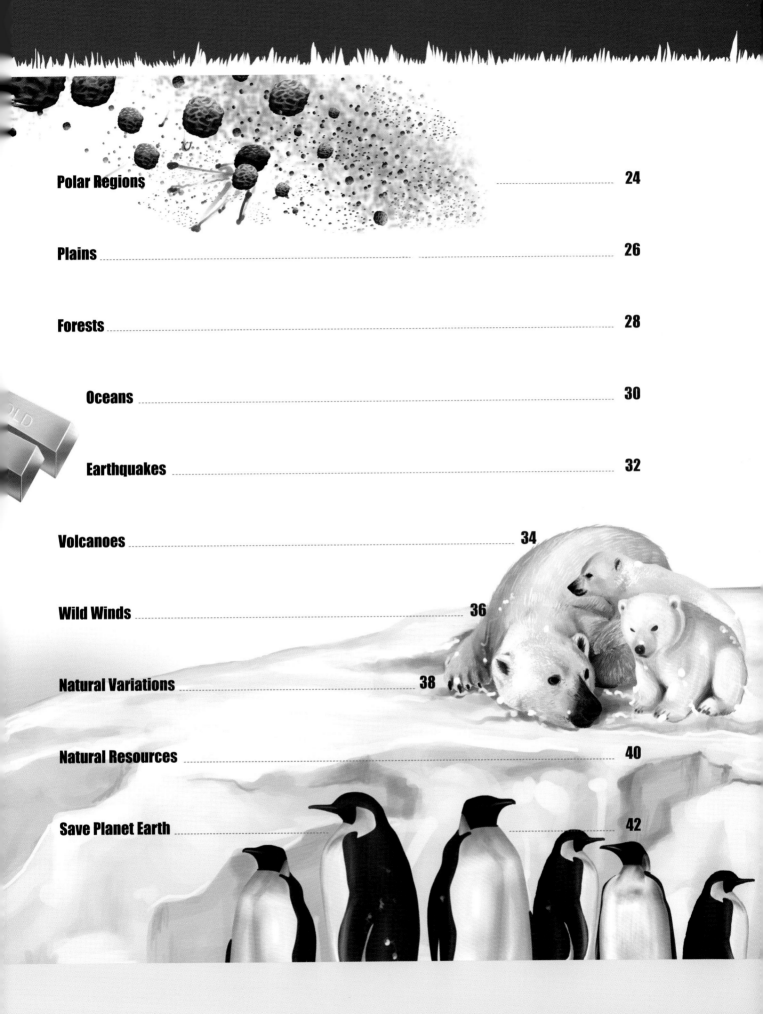

About the Earth

In our solar system there are eight planets and the Sun. Earth is the 3rd planet as per it's distance from the Sun. It is the fifth largest planet and looks blue from space.

Earth is the only known living planet in the universe. Earth is home for millions of species including humans. It's about 5 billion years old and within it's first billion years of formation, life appeared on Earth's surface. About 71% of the surface is covered by life giving water and the rest by continents and islands.

The blue planet ▶

Sun

Mercury

Venus

Earth

Mars

Earth's interior is divided into three layers — A thick layer of solid mantle, a liquid outer core generating magnetic field and solid iron inner core. Earth's surface has several rigid segments or tectonic plates which are slowly but constantly moving.

The Earth is a sphere, tilted about 230° on it's axis and rotating, thus resulting in seasons. It revolves around the Sun in about 365.26 days. The Moon is it's only natural satellite which revolves around it, creating oceanic tides and stabilizing the axial tilt.

Saturn

Neptune

Uranus

Jupiter

Birth of the Earth

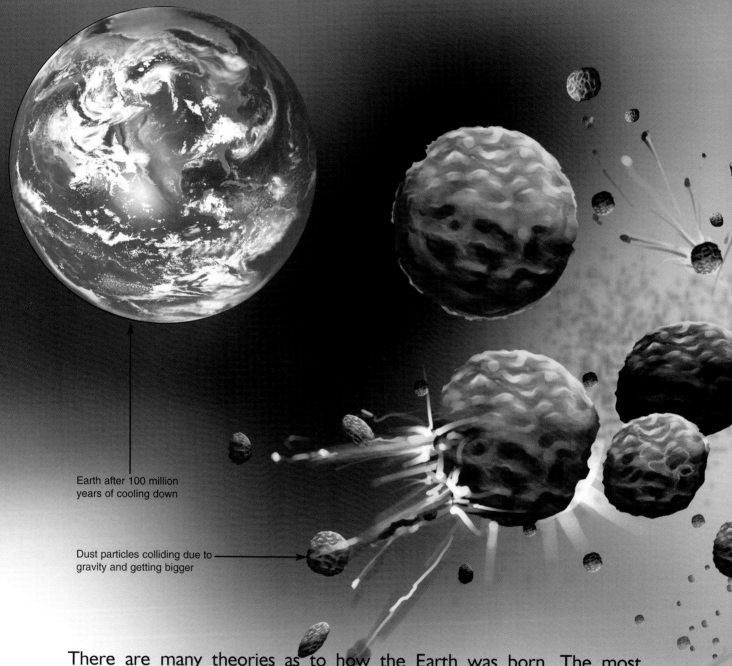

Earth after 100 million years of cooling down

Dust particles colliding due to gravity and getting bigger

There are many theories as to how the Earth was born. The most commonly accepted one is that the solar system began when a huge old star exploded and heavy elements like carbon, lithium, etc. flew off in to space and got mixed with hydrogen. The mixture of these gases became a nebula from which the Earth and other planets were formed.

Gradually, the rapidly expanding nebula cooled down, contracted and started spinning and became a disk called the solar nebula.

Most of the mass concentrated at the centre, resulting in pressure and creating a lot of heat, thus the liquid core.

Away from the centre, where it was cooler, a whirlpool formed, the debris became sand like grains, collided and stuck together. Bit by bit this built up the huge mass of the planets. It is estimated to have taken about 100 million years to complete the formation of the Earth.

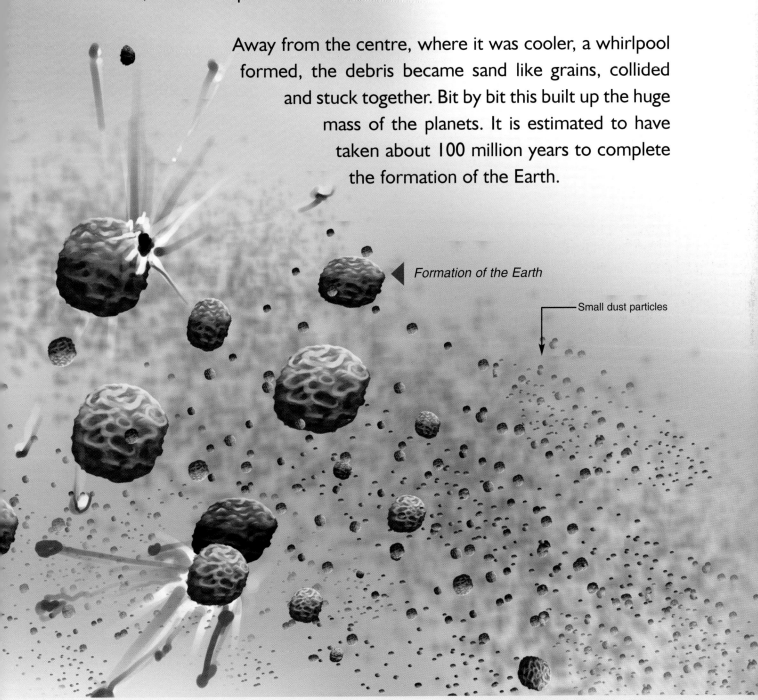

Formation of the Earth

Small dust particles

Composition of the Earth

The Earth is rocky unlike other planets, which are largely gaseous. It is considerably large with the highest density, strongest gravity and the strongest magnetic field amongst the other planets, in our solar system.

Shape

The Earth is not a perfect sphere. It has a unique shape called a geoid. It rotates at a high speed, creating a bulge around its equator. The length of the equator is thus longer than the distance between the two poles.

The highest point on the surface of the Earth is Mount Everest (8,848 metres above sea level) and the lowest is Mariana Trench (10,911 metres below sea level).

Inside the Earth

Broadly distinguishing, it has three layers divided chemically. The Crust is where we stand. It is a thin cover, most of which is under the ocean as the Earth is covered majorly by water and rest as continents.

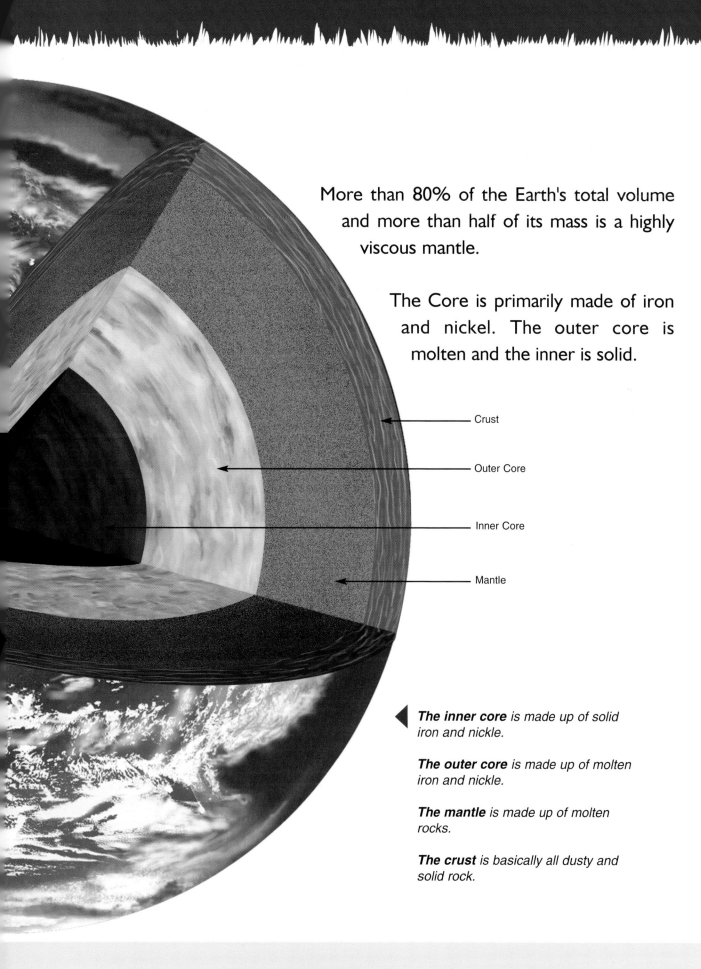

More than 80% of the Earth's total volume and more than half of its mass is a highly viscous mantle.

The Core is primarily made of iron and nickel. The outer core is molten and the inner is solid.

Crust

Outer Core

Inner Core

Mantle

The inner core is made up of solid iron and nickle.

The outer core is made up of molten iron and nickle.

The mantle is made up of molten rocks.

The crust is basically all dusty and solid rock.

Shifting Continents

There are seven continents in the world today. They are Asia, Europe, North America, South America, Africa, Australia and Antarctia. They are separated by vast water bodies called Oceans. But it was not always like this. Around 220 million years ago it was a huge single super continent called Pangaea. As the Earth's crust was always moving the Pangaea broke into two continents — Laurasia in the north and Gondwanaland in the south. This breaking process continued and eventually the seven continents came into being. The continents are still moving at the rate of approximately 2 mm in a month. This shift in continents explains how totally different lands with very diverse conditions have the same fossils. There are similarities in rocks found in Namibia in Africa and Brazil in South America and so on. By the same logic, millions of years from now the Earth might end up looking completely different from what it is at present. Continents may merge or segregate from each other. Oceans may become larger or disappear altogether.

Permian period was around 250 million years ago. Permian lasted for approximately 40 million years. Land was mostly covered

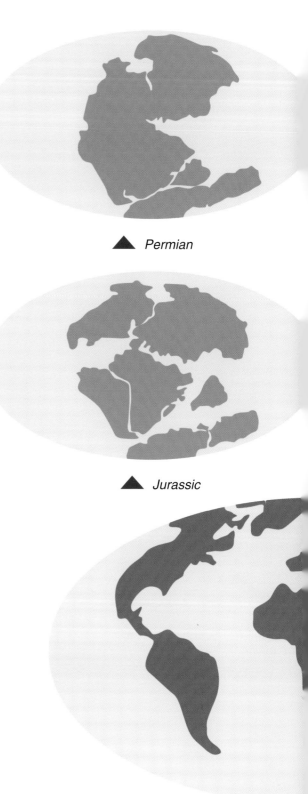

▲ *Permian*

▲ *Jurassic*

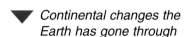

Triassic

Cretaceous

Earth today

with forests and the trees almost used to look like dwarf pine trees. The fossils of these trees in present have become the largest source of coal.

Triassic was around 200 million years ago. It is difficult to say for exactly how many million years this era lasted. Corals made their first appearance on Earth during this time. So did some flowering plants and the first flying vertebrates.

The Jurassic period was around 135 million years ago. It is popularly remembered as the 'age of dinosaurs'. The Jurassic was named so because of the exposure of the Jura Mountains, where Germany, Switzerland and France meet today. A lot of fishes and sea reptiles evolved during this period. Because of the warm and humid atmosphere of the Earth, lush green jungles were formed with large trees.

The Cretaceous period was approximately 65 million years ago. A lot of animals and plants came to an extinction. Thus this period is also called the era of mass extinction. Scientists say that most of the amphibians of this era survived and are evolving till date. Most importantly, by the end of this era more land surfaced and there was a huge downfall in the sea level.

Orbit and Rotation of the Earth

The Earth rotates from east to west on its axis. While doing so, one half of the Earth faces the Sun and the other half faces away from the Sun, thus causing day and night respectively. Earth completes one rotation in 24 hours which is why we have 24 hours in a day.

Different parts of the world have different times of the day at exactly the same moment. When people in Asia start their day in the morning, Europeans go to sleep and people in eastern United States of America have their evening tea at the same moment.

▼ *Rotation causing day and night*

Night

Day

Ancient people like the Egyptians had their own beliefs about the existence of night and day. Nicolaus Copernicus in 1543 first published the correct theory about the Earth orbiting the Sun, thereby causing night and day.

While standing on the crust of the Earth we do not feel that it is moving. But the Earth is constantly revolving around the Sun at a speed of 30 km/sec

▲ *Winter*

▲ *Summer*

while rotating on its axis. It takes approximately 365.25 days to make a full circle around the Sun from a distance of 150 million km away from it on its orbit. As the path of the orbit is not a perfect circle but an oval shape, therefore the Earth is closer to the Sun at one point than another. It's closest point is called the perihelion (happens around January) and its furthest point is called aphelion (happens around July).

▲ *Oval orbit of Earth with the Sun in the centre.*
Diagram showing revolution of the Earth on its orbit
around the Sun, causing summer and winter

Seasons

The Earth does not spin upright. It is tilted at an angle. When the Earth is on one side of the Sun and the northern hemisphere is tilted towards the Sun, it gets more sunlight and thus experiences summer. At the same time, the southern hemisphere is tilted away from the Sun bringing winter. Similarly when the southern hemisphere is tilted towards the Sun it's summer and winter in the northern hemisphere.

In between, neither hemisphere is tilted more towards the Sun. They are known as the Equinoxes (the Longest Day, the Longest Night — one in July, other in September), when both hemispheres receive equal sunlight and cause spring and autumn, which is neither too hot nor too cold. This is how we have seasons around the world. Depending on the location of any place on the Earth it has longer or shorter seasons.

Besides, mountains and oceans also influence seasons and the climate of a

▼ Spring

▼ Winter

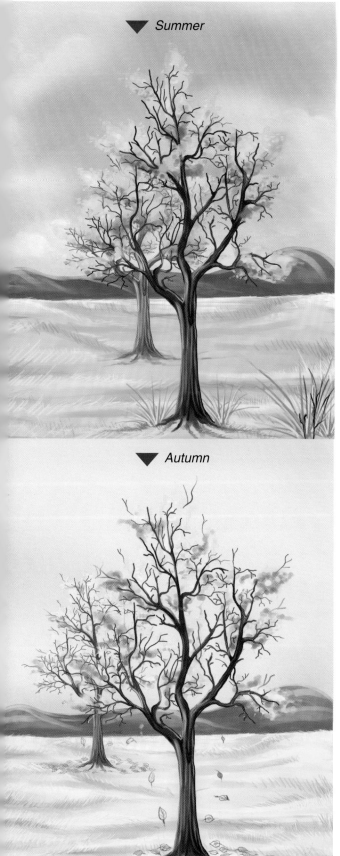

▼ *Summer*

▼ *Autumn*

particular place. Places near equators getting direct sunlight are hot, coastal areas are cooler, polar zones like the Arctic and Antarctic are extremely cold as they do not receive direct sunlight.

There are four primary seasons which are more prominent in the north and south of the world. They are Spring, Summer, Autumn and Winter. Spring, which comes after Winter brings the cheer of new life. New buds start appearing on trees followed by formation of new leaves and the trees turning lush and green. Summers are majorly hot and dry and are followed by monsoons. Monsoon is mostly referred to as an Asiatic phenomenon which brings heavy rains and high humidity. It helps in rice plantation. Monsoon also causes severe damage to roads and houses due to mudslides along the hills. The days gradually become cooler in Autumn and leaves of most trees change to red and yellow. Then the leaves fall down indicating the onset of Winter. During Winter trees go bare and many animals also sleep through the entire season. This is called hibernation.

Magnetic Field of the Earth

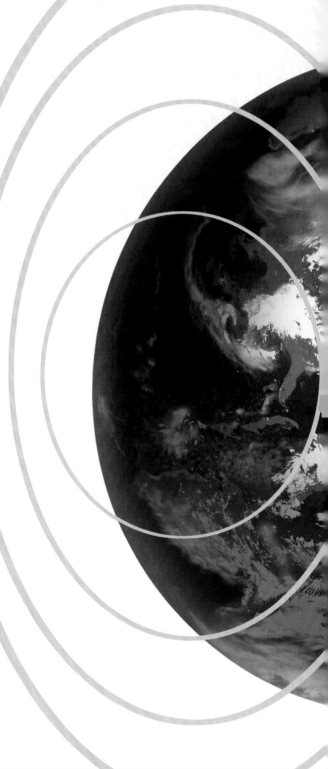

The motion of electric charges produces a magnetic field. Earth's magnetic field is explained by what is called a dynamo effect. The inner core is made of iron and nickel, the outer core is liquid. The spinning liquid produces electrical currents by the coupling of convective effects and rotation. The resulting rocks from this molten state contain indicators of this magnetic field. These rocks are magnetic fossils which also indicates that the Earth's magnetic field reverses itself every million years or so.

Thus there is a switch of north and south magnetic poles. Details of this theory are still to be established.

Earth's magnetosphere represents a region of space dominated by the Earth's magnetic field. A stream of ionised gases blows from the Sun at about 400 km/sec. As it encounters the magnetosphere it is deflected, thus gets prevented from entering the Earth.

◄ Diagram showing the Earth as a magnet with its magnetic field. Due to this magnetic field some intense electro-magnetic rays from the Sun are repelled back into space, prohibiting them from entering the Earth's surface.

Atmosphere

In the beginning Earth didn't have any atmosphere as the atmospheric gases were blown away into space by the solar wind. Gradually when the Earth cooled down and started shrinking, a huge amount of pressure formed in the mantle and it squeezed the gases out of the rocks. This mixture of hydrogen, helium, methane and ammonia created the first atmosphere. But this got lost into space as Earth's gravity was not strong enough to hold these gases. Simultaneously, the molten rocks started releasing heavier gases like carbon dioxide and nitrogen with water vapour. When the Sun's rays hit these, there were

Harmful rays from the Sun being reflected by the Ozone layer

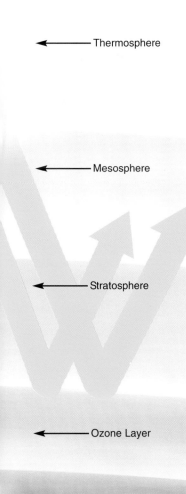

Thermosphere

Mesosphere

Stratosphere

Ozone Layer

Troposphere

considerable changes. The steam rose up, then cooled down, condensed into continuous rain for a long period of time. This led to the formation of the Oceans.

Gradually, the lava emerging out of the mountains settled slowly to form the continents.

At present the atmosphere is made up of five layers — Troposphere, Stratosphere, Mesosphere, Thermosphere and Exosphere. These layers have different composition and density of gases.

Mountains

Mountains are landforms that stand at least 1,000 feet above the surroundings on land. They differ in size and age. Some are isolated peaks, volcanic in nature. Some others form a series of elevated rocky surfaces called mountain range.

A mountain seems solid and unchanging, but they are also changing due to continental shifts. The Himalaya is the youngest and is still growing. Whereas New York's Adirondads or India's Aravalli are old and have been reduced down to hills.

Mountains are formed when the plates of the Earth's crust

▲ Snow-capped mountains melt and produce streams of water, which later forms lakes, ponds, and rivers.

push one another. They are also formed when deposits accumulate over a period of time.

24% of Earth's land is covered by mountains. Most of the world's rivers are formed from mountains. More than half of the human population of the Earth depends on mountains for water as life resource.

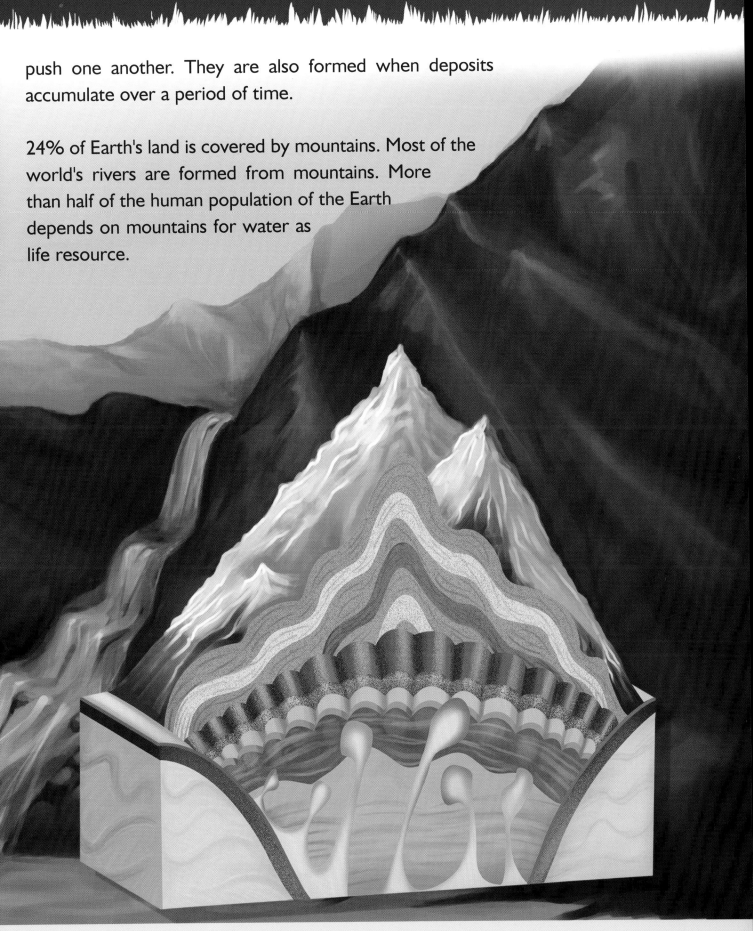

▲ *Diagram showing how constant folding of rocks forms a mountain*

Deserts

A desert is a place where water is scarce. It receives less than 10 inches of rain annually. It may or may not be covered by sand and not all deserts are hot. One seventh's of Earth's land surface is desert. They are found in all the continents, including Antarctica.

Usually deserts are hot during the day as there are no clouds to prevent the Sun's rays to fall directly on the surface. They are very cold during the night.

The cool clouds containing water vapours travel far from the desert due to a typical pressure making it dry and hot, thus producing lesser rain which in turn makes the hot air surrounding the area of the deserts very dry. Only thorny shrubs and dry grasses survive on deserts.

Cactus

Tarantula

Life in a desert

Camel

Desert Lizard

Desert Snake

Scorpion

Desert Tortoise

An Oasis is a special area found in deserts. It is a water source with a pond in the middle of anywhere in the desert. Green vegetation surrounds this pond and also provides a good healthy natural habitat for many animals and often human beings. Oasis are formed by underground rivers. The low pressure in the atmosphere results the water to

An Oasis

come up and form a pond. The most important plant in an oasis is the Date Palm. It is very important as it holds the soil firmly and provides shade to other plants from the burning Sun. Other important plants that farmers grow in an Oasis are potatos, onions, carrots, olives and figs.

Al-Hasa in Saudi Arabia is the world's largest Oasis known to us till date. Then there are other Oasis like Al-Qatif-E in Gedi in Israel, Farafra in Egypt, Kufra in Libya. Very interestingly Las Vegas valley in United States was also once upon a time an Oasis of Mojave Deserts.

In deserts we often find a cluster of humans. They are nomadic in nature, and live in temporary canvas tents with their cattle and families. They travel from one part of the desert to another in search of vegetation and water.

23

Polar Regions

The icy areas around the Earth's north and south poles are the Polar Regions.

The northern polar region is called the Arctic, the word being derived from the Greek word *Arktos*, which means Bear. The Arctic region consists of a vast ice-covered ocean surrounded by treeless, frozen ground. Average winter temperatures are as low as -40°C. Precipitation is mostly in the form of snow. The vegetation is of mainly dwarf shrubs, herbs, lichens and mosses, all growing near the ground, forming the tundra. Herbivores on the tundra are the Arctic hare, muskbox, lemmings, etc. The most famous predator is the Polar Bear.

▲ *A community of Seals*

The Arctic has natural resources like oil and gas. The scientists are highly cautious of the fact that the ice on the Arctic is melting at a fast rate due to global warming, resulting in subsequent increase in sea levels which might further lead to the continental submerge.

The southern pole is called Antarctica. It gets its name from the fact that there are no Polar Bears to be found here, thus Anti Arctic or Antarctic. It is the fifth largest continent in the world. It is totally covered by ice. It is the coldest, driest and windiest of the continents. Only animals and plants adapted to extreme cold climate can survive here. Few animals and plants of this region are penguins, seals, mosses and algae. Antarctica belongs to no country.

▲ *Polar Bear*

▲ *Emperor Penguins*

Plains

A plain is an area of land which is broad and flat. They occur at lowlands and at the bottom of valleys, but also on plateaus at high elevations. In general it is a land no more than 1,000 feet above the sea level.

There are various types of plains depending on their location, vegetation and soil. A Coastal Plain is adjacent to a sea-cost, and it could be a part of the elevated ocean floor. The Atlantic Coastal Plain is a fertile and well populated land.

A Flood Plain is the floor of a river valley beyond the river bed. It consists of mud, sand and silt which are left behind when the river overflows its banks.

Alluvial Plains form over a long period of time by a river depositing sediments which becomes alluvial soil.

Lacustrine Plain is formed in a Lacustrine (Latin word *Lacus* meaning *Lake*) environment that means it is the sedimentary environment of a lake.

Till Plains (till is glacial sediment) are formed when a sheet of ice is detached from a glacier, and when it melts, that place has a deposit of sediments which were being carried by it. Lava Plains are formed by sheets of lava.

Plant life on plains is controlled by the climate. If it is humid we have thick forests. In dry areas we have grasslands. Plains are usually well populated as the soil and terrain are good for farming.

▲ *Landscape of a plain*

Forests

A forest is an area consisting of many trees and supporting many life forms. The type of trees in an area defines a special environment for the typical kinds of animals and other living creatures to live and co-exist. Forests covers 30% of the total land. Forests help in water preservation, circulation and also prevent soil erosion. They provide fuelwood, fodder and many other things on which human life depends. Forests are broadly classified as follows:

Tropical Rainforests

They get rain the whole year round. The temperature is high because of being close to the equator and rain results in dense, lush forests. They are home to two thirds of all living animals and plant species on the planet. The undergrowth is restricted as very little sunlight touches the ground. The huge leaves cover the head of the trees of the forest forming a canopy. The largest tropical rainforest exists in the Amazon region. The space between the canopy and forest floor is called understorey. This is home to a large number of birds, snakes, lizards, jaguars, leopards and insects.

▼ *A Tropical forest*

Subtropical Forests

The summers are hot and winters are warm in these forests. Palms, citrus and many broad-leaf evergreens flourish in this zone.

Tropical Forests

Tropical forests have a tropical climate that is warm to hot and moist year-round. They mostly have lush vegetation but are also found in alpine tundra, snow-capped regions and in areas with extreme heat such as the Sahara desert.

▲ *A Rainforest*

Coniferous Forests

Conifer means 'needle-like' and the trees include cedars, firs, junipers, pine, etc. An area characterised by coniferous forests is Taiga. Covering most of Alaska, Canada, Sweden, Russia, northern Kazakhasthan and Japan, the Taiga is the largest Terrestrial biome.

Mediterranean Forests

Mediterranean forests are evergreen forests around the coasts of the Mediterranean, California, Chile and Western Australia. The trees are mixed hardwood and softwood. They have hot, dry summers and mild rainy winters.

Oceans

In the beginning, the Earth was dry. It was also very hot. The volcanic steam and dust filled up the Earth and it's atmosphere. This helped and protected Earth from the blaze of the Sun and slowly the Earth cooled down. This steam and dust then condensed into rain. The rain lasted for thousands of years creating vast oceans and giving the Earth it's name — the blue planet.

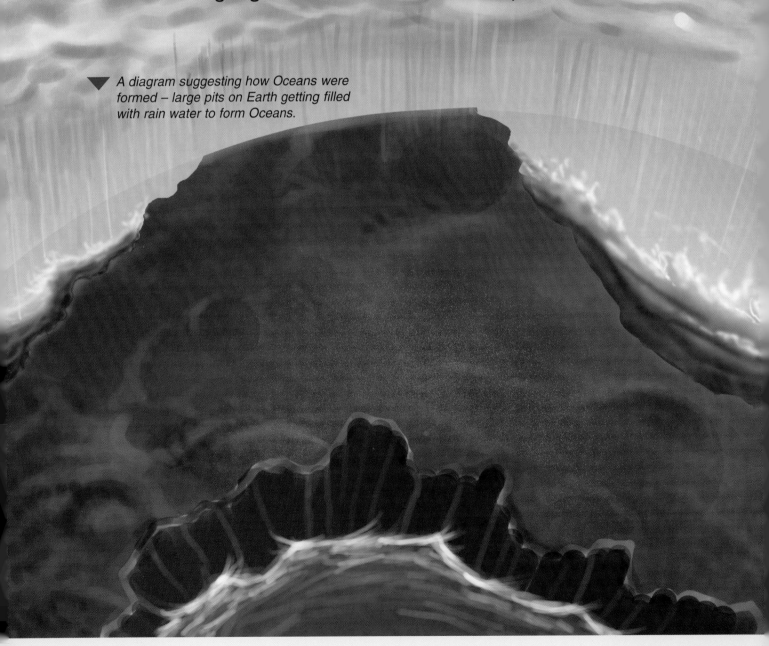

▼ A diagram suggesting how Oceans were formed – large pits on Earth getting filled with rain water to form Oceans.

There are five great oceans. They are the Atlantic, Arctic, Indian Ocean, Pacific Ocean and Southern Ocean. Together they cover more than 70% of the Earth's surface. Pacific Ocean is the biggest. It is twice as large as the Atlantic. It covers an area which is almost two thirds of the world.

On an average, oceans are about 2,000 metres deep. On the floor of an ocean are the oceanic trenches. Trenches are made with tectonic plates and are driven down into the mantle. The deepest trench is the Mariana Trench. It is 10,863 metres deep.

Oceanic tides are the rise and fall of the ocean due to the Moon's gravitational force on the Earth. They are called high tides and low tides. During high tide the water gradually moves towards the seashore and during low tides it retreats back slowly. It happens twice every day. Salt constitutes 3.5% of total mass of the ocean. Ocean water is saline, which is why 97% of water on Earth is saline and the rest is fresh water.

Fresh water mainly comes from the ice. Salt in the ocean is due to volcanic activity and from igneous rocks. The dissolved atmospheric gases help in the survival of various aquatic life forms. Oceans act as a huge heat reservoir and influence the world's climate.

Oceans are home to approximatly 60% of the living species on our planet. The first life was formed in the ocean and we are still exploring this vast reservoir for newer species even today.

Earthquakes

The rigid segments on the Earth's crust or the tectonic plates are slowly and constantly moving. If during the movements one plate slips past the other, it causes minor shakes or tremors. They are mild and do not last long. But if they get jammed, pressure builds up until they get segregated and move on. This results in massive vibrations in all directions. It starts from a point of origin and the waves of the vibration radiate out in circles called hypocenter of focus. Vibrations become weaker as they gradually move out farther from the centre.

Earthquakes generally do not last more than a minute. The longest known earthquake happened in Alaska and it lasted for 4 minutes. Earthquakes which take place below the ocean on the ocean beds result in tsunamis. Tsunamis are huge waves and cause extreme damage.

Scientists studying earthquakes are called seismologists. They use a device called seismograph to grade the scale of the earthquake. Measurement techniques were first developed by the Chinese some 2000 years ago.

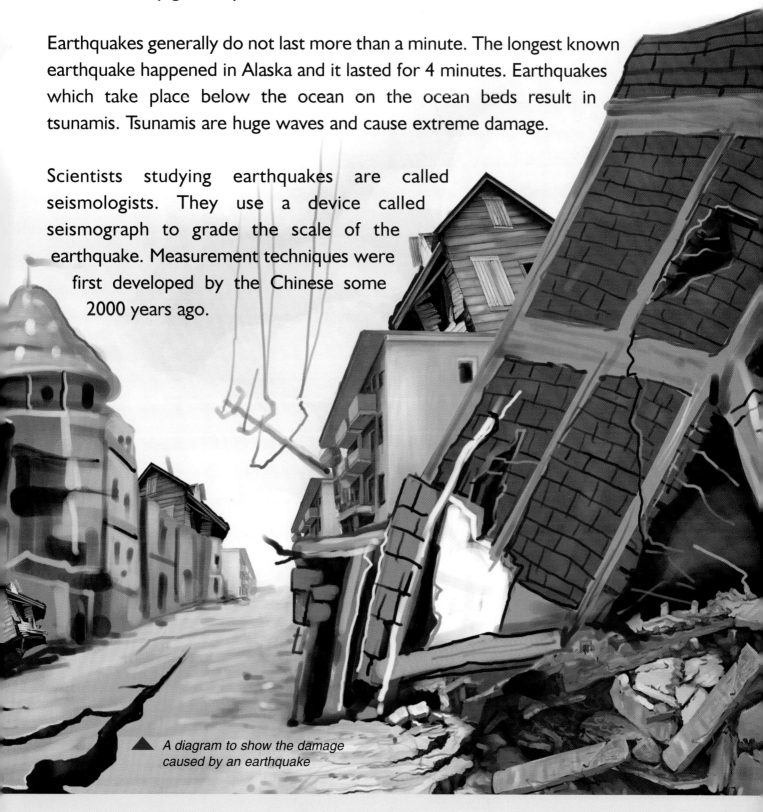

A diagram to show the damage caused by an earthquake

Volcanoes

The rocks deep inside Earth's crust are so hot that they are in a molten state. These molten rocks or magma rise to the surface due to huge pressure and try to escape along a break or vent near the peak of the mountain. This sudden eruption and gigantic explosion sends up jets of steam, rocks, magma and ash in the air which is then called lava. Volcanoes are mountains containing lava and volcanic eruptions are when the volcano erupts. If successive eruptions occur, they build up a huge cone of ash and lava, building new mountains in few months.

The clouds of smoke that come out of the crater are made of steam and smelly sulphurous gases. The hot lava is thrown high into the air and gradually solidifies as it falls to Earth.

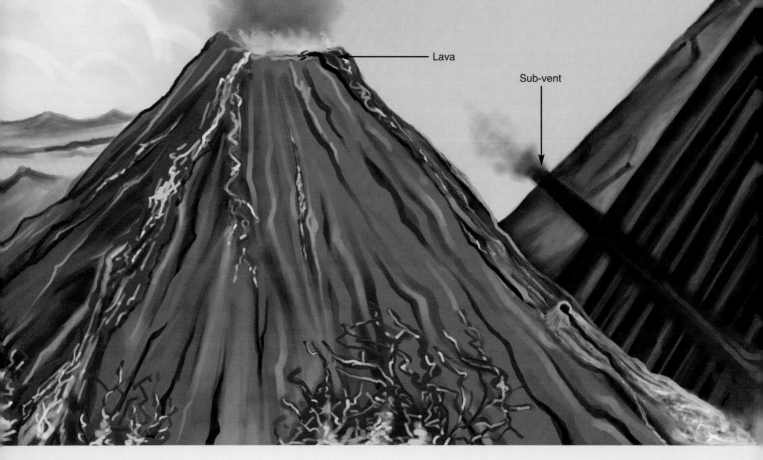

Lava

Sub-vent

Frothy lava cools and hardens into pumice stone which has lots of air bubbles caught inside. Volcanic ash is fine particles of dust blown into the air and settled all around the mountain.

Volcanoes that erupt regularly are active. If a volcano has not erupted in 100 years, it is called sleeping or dormant volcano. But if there are no signs of eruption for thousands of years, they are known as extinct volcanoes.

Sometimes the magma erupts underneath the water, making the lava build up a volcano, whose peak rises above the surface of the ocean to form an island.

Main Vent

Diagram showing what happens inside a volcano during an eruption

Magma

Wild Winds

Air is all around us. Wind is the movement of air. When the Sun warms a particular place, air expands and becomes lighter. It rises leaving an area of low air pressure near the ground. Surrounding cool air, which is under higher pressure rushes to replace the rising air and this movement makes wind. Once the air has risen, warmer air becomes cool and heavy again. It sinks alongside the rising air and creates a high pressure area near the ground. The greater the difference in air pressure between the two areas, the stronger the winds that blow. This can lead to mild winds becoming wild winds. Gradually, the strong winds can turn out to be storms.

Thunderstorms

They are built up on warm or hot humid days or along a cold front. Inside a very big cloud huge raindrops grow. Whirlwinds within the clouds hurl the drops together very violently, resulting in static electricity. This charge gets released with massive flashes of lightning.

Tornado

If violently spinning air forms the shape of a funnel beneath a thundercloud swooping towards the ground, there occurs an area of low pressure at the centre. This centre sucks up everything in its path and tosses everything into the air at a very high speed like toys. These storms are called tornadoes. They can move at a speed of 400 km/hr. This usually happens around the month of March to July in Midwest America. which is also called Tornado Alley.

▲ *Hurricane*

Hurricane

They are huge tropical storms which develop over the eastern Atlantic Ocean. The storm then moves towards the east coast of America. While raging over the warm ocean the storm gets lots of heat and water vapour making it even stronger. It spins at a great speed of 320 km/hr forming a calm centre called the 'eye'. It carries strong and tall waves to the surface causing huge damages. In the year 1963, Hurricane Flora killed 6,000 people in the Caribbean.

Hailstorms

They are storms precipitating chunks of ice. They usually occur during regular thunderstorms. But there have been reports of hail larger than 2 inches in diameter causing much damage and injuries. In 1988, a hailstorm killed 246 people in India.

Tornado

Natural Variations

Rocks

The hard mass of the Earth's surface is made of rocks. There are primarily three types of rocks.

▲ Metamorphic rock

Metamorphic rocks are formed when other types of rocks suffer extreme heat and pressure, e.g. limestone under heat and pressure converts into marble.

Igneous rocks are formed out of cooled magma.

▲ Igneous rock

Sedimentary rocks are formed on seabeds and are in layers.

The hot magma also leads to the formation of gems.

▲ Sedimentary rock

Lakes and Rivers

Only 3% of water on Earth is freshwater which is found in the form of ice, rivers, lakes and also as underground water. When the snow melts in the mountains, the water flows down in the form of rivers, which then meet the sea. Initially, the water in the river flows very fast and as it nears the sea, it slows down and forms deltas. Rivers create many tributaries and may even join other rivers along their way. Lakes are filled with silt of slow moving water. They are formed in huge depressions on the surface of the Earth. If lakes have a stream or outward flow of groundwater, it is called a fresh or open lake. Lake Baikal in Russia is the world's deepest lake.

Clouds

When surface water is warmed by the Sun, water turns into water vapour and rises into the air. When the air cools, the vapour condenses into tiny droplets and if it is cooled further, into bits of ice. These are called clouds. Depending on

▼ Cumulonimbus

▼ Cirrus

▼ Cumulus

▼ Stratus

the height and the air that they form in, clouds are classified into various types and are given different names. **Cirrus clouds** are fine and wispy. They are made of ice crystals being extremely high in the sky (above 18,000 feet). They are blown into long streams and predict pleasant weather.

Cumulus are fluffy clouds. They form when warm air rises and cools. They look like floating cotton. If they grow upward they turn into giant **Cumulonimbus clouds**, which result in thunderstorms. **Stratus** clouds are low clouds. They make the sky look dull and grey. They cover the entire sky like a blanket. They mostly result in light drizzles or mist.

Snow

Stream

River

Open Lake

Ocean

Delta

Lake

Natural Resources

Natural Resources are valuable or precious substances found naturally on the Earth. They are our natural assets. They can be valuable in the way man puts them to use and are classified as renewable or non-renewable.

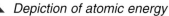

▲ *Depiction of atomic energy*

Renewable resources are usually biological products like food, wood, forests, etc, which can renew themselves if they are not over extracted or over used.

They are self sustainable if used prudently by us. Non-living renewable resources are soil, water, oxygen, etc. Renewable fuel resources are the power sources from solar, wind, geothermal, etc. They do not need regeneration.

A non-renewable resource is ideally that which exists in a limited amount, cannot be remade, re-grown or regenerated as fast as compared to the speed in which it is consumed by human beings. They are majorly the various kinds of fuels that are used like coal, petroleum, natural gases, etc. They take an extremely long time to renew.

On the basis of origin, resources are also divided as follows:

Abiotic

Abiotic resources comprise of non-living things, e.g. land, water, air and minerals such as gold, iron, copper, etc.

▲ *Wind energy*

Hydro energy

Biotic

Biotic resources are derived from the biosphere of the Earth, forests and their products, animals, birds, fish, marine organisms, also minerals like coal and petroleum as they are formed from decayed organic matter.

Fossil fuel ▶

They can also be divided on the basis of the stages of development like:

Potential Resources

Potential Resources are those existing in a region which can be used in the future, e.g. mineral oil may exist at places having sedimentary rocks but they remain potential till they are actually drilled and extracted.

◀ *Coal and Dimonds*

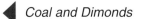
▼ *Solar energy*

Actual Resources

Actual resources are the ones which have been studied as per their quality and quantity. Hence, they have been determined through technology and the extraction cost has been calculated. The profitable part of such resources is called reserves.

Gold ▶

Save Planet Earth

Earth is home to human beings and many other living creatures. But in nature, animals and plants only consume as per their basic needs. Man is the only creature who not only consumes but accumulates, resulting in greed. Driven by greed of accumulating more and the fear of losing it all, man stoops down to the lowest level of extortion and damages beyond repair.

But as and when awareness grew we understood the interdependency on each other to survive on this planet. Though there have been many irreversible damages, man is still trying to learn and lessen the harm done to Mother Earth. Some of the shocking revelations are:

1. Arctic has warmed by 3°C and is melting three weeks earlier than before. The overall rate of glacier melt has accelerated. As the amount of ice flowing into the sea has doubled, so has the level of the sea, resulting in increase in temperature, causing the oceans to expand. These are causing Hurricanes more frequently, which are more devastating than ever before. The reason

behind this whole phenomenon is the Earth's temperature which has risen because of greenhouse effect due to burning of fossil fuels, e.g. coal, fuel and natural gas used for everyday purposes.

European heat waves and sudden changes in climate across the globe are also due to the same reason.

2. Excessive industrial wastes are being dumped indiscriminately in the water bodies without even proper treatment for toxicity, which is resulting in destruction of massive water bodies, also making them toxic and therefore unfit for any life existing in them. It is also resulting in many congenital deformities in humans due to consumption of poisonous water.

3. Landslides are frequent and mountains are getting damaged due to massive deforestation and also unregulated mining and various resources extraction activities. This is not only changing the surface of the Earth but also leading to soil erosion which can have severe repercussions on the agricultural produce and natural resources.

Reprinted in 2015

An imprint of Om Books International

Corporate & Editorial Office
A 12, Sector 64, Noida 201 301
Uttar Pradesh, India
Phone: +91 120 477 4100
Email: editorial@ombooks.com
Website: www.ombooksinternational.com

Sales Office
107, Ansari Road, Darya Ganj, New Delhi 110 002, India
Phone: +91 11 4000 9000, 2326 3363, 2326 5303
Fax: +91 11 2327 8091
Email: sales@ombooks.com
Website: www.ombooks.com

Art Editor: Rachna Panchal

ISBN: 978-81-87108-94-8

Printed in India

10 9 8 7 6 5 4 3 2